Rosès and Rufus

WILD BOO..

sloth

written and illustrated by

Clare Beaton

b small publishing
www.bsmall.co.uk

The Wild

dung beetle

homerus swallowtail butterfly

Wild creatures live in natural environments finding food, water and shelter without help from humans. In some parts of the world, deforestation, pollution, hunting, farming and draining of land threaten these natural environments.

Many countries create wildlife sanctuaries or national parks to protect wild animals and their habitats. But as the human population increases, the once untouched wild parts of the planet decrease and many wild creatures and plants lose their homes.

In urban areas, some wild animals such as foxes and raccoons have adapted to life. Zoos, which used to capture and display wild animals for the public, now focus on protecting endangered species and reintroducing them into the wild.

flamingo

red and green macaw

coconut palm tree

Activities

Each topic in this book comes with a simple craft activity or yummy recipe for you to enjoy at home. Here are some helpful tips to get you started.

Materials

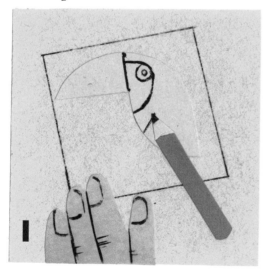

It's useful to have some materials ready such as cereal and tissue boxes, thicker card and card tubes for when you feel creative.

Several activities in this book use recycled items and perhaps you could think of some more ideas.

Templates

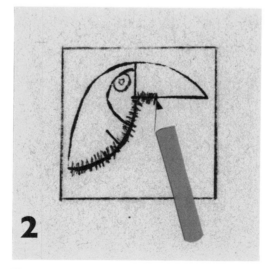

1 Place a piece of tracing paper over the template. Hold steady and draw around the shape.

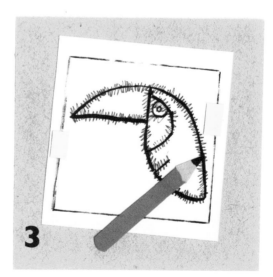

2 Turn the tracing paper over and scribble over the lines with a soft pencil.

3 Turn over again and tape to paper or card. Retrace firmly over the original lines. Remove tracing paper.

TIP You can use greaseproof paper instead of tracing paper.

3

Friendly Giants

Elephants are the largest land animal. The African elephant is bigger than the Indian elephant. Both have a long trunk, which they use for breathing, holding things and washing themselves. Their ivory tusks are magnificent and continue to grow all their lives.

Living in groups led by older females, elephants are very intelligent and have strong family bonds. Their memory is excellent and they never forget. They are vegetarian, love water and can live for up to seventy years in the wild. Poaching for their tusks, habitat loss and conflict with humans are threatening the elephant population.

Böhm's
bee-eater

African elephant

rhino

elephant template

Elephants encore!

Elephants sometimes walk in a line holding the tail of the one in front with their trunk.

What you will need:
Piece of A4 paper, scissors, ruler, pencil, tracing paper, sticky tape, felt-tip pens.

1. Cut a strip of paper 9 cm wide and 27 cm long. Fold into three.

2. Trace elephant template (see instructions on page 3) on top of folded paper keeping the fold on the right.
3. Holding carefully together, cut out just along dotted line.
4. Unfold, draw over traced lines in pen and repeat on the other two pieces.
5. Colour and decorate. Write a message on the back.

TIP You can add more elephants to make a long line. Stick together with tape on the back.

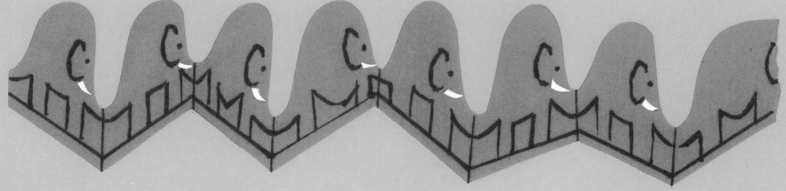

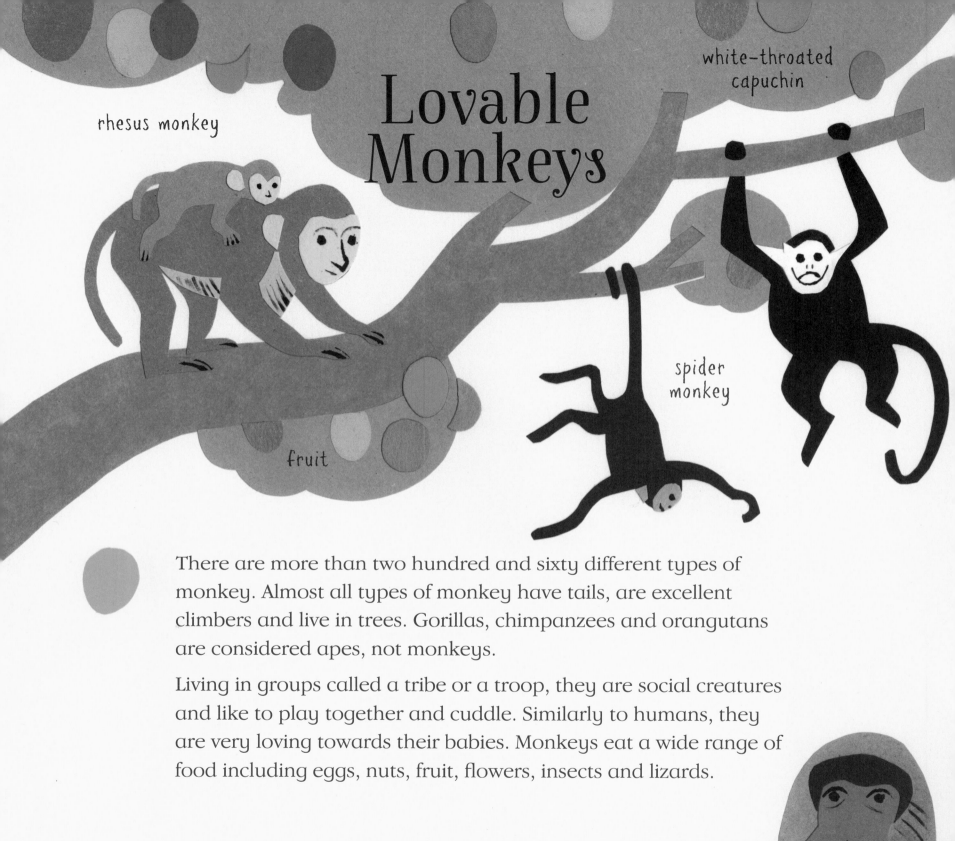

Lovable Monkeys

rhesus monkey

white-throated capuchin

spider monkey

fruit

proboscis monkey

There are more than two hundred and sixty different types of monkey. Almost all types of monkey have tails, are excellent climbers and live in trees. Gorillas, chimpanzees and orangutans are considered apes, not monkeys.

Living in groups called a tribe or a troop, they are social creatures and like to play together and cuddle. Similarly to humans, they are very loving towards their babies. Monkeys eat a wide range of food including eggs, nuts, fruit, flowers, insects and lizards.

6

Fruit basket

What you will need:
Thin coloured card, pencil, tracing paper, scissors, ruler, knife, glue.

1. Trace the basket template (see instructions on page 3) on card. Cut out.
2. Place on flat surface and score lightly with knife along ruler following the dotted lines.
3. Fold along scored lines.
4. Glue the two side flaps at one end to the inside edge of the short side panel and hold firmly until glued together, then repeat at the other end.

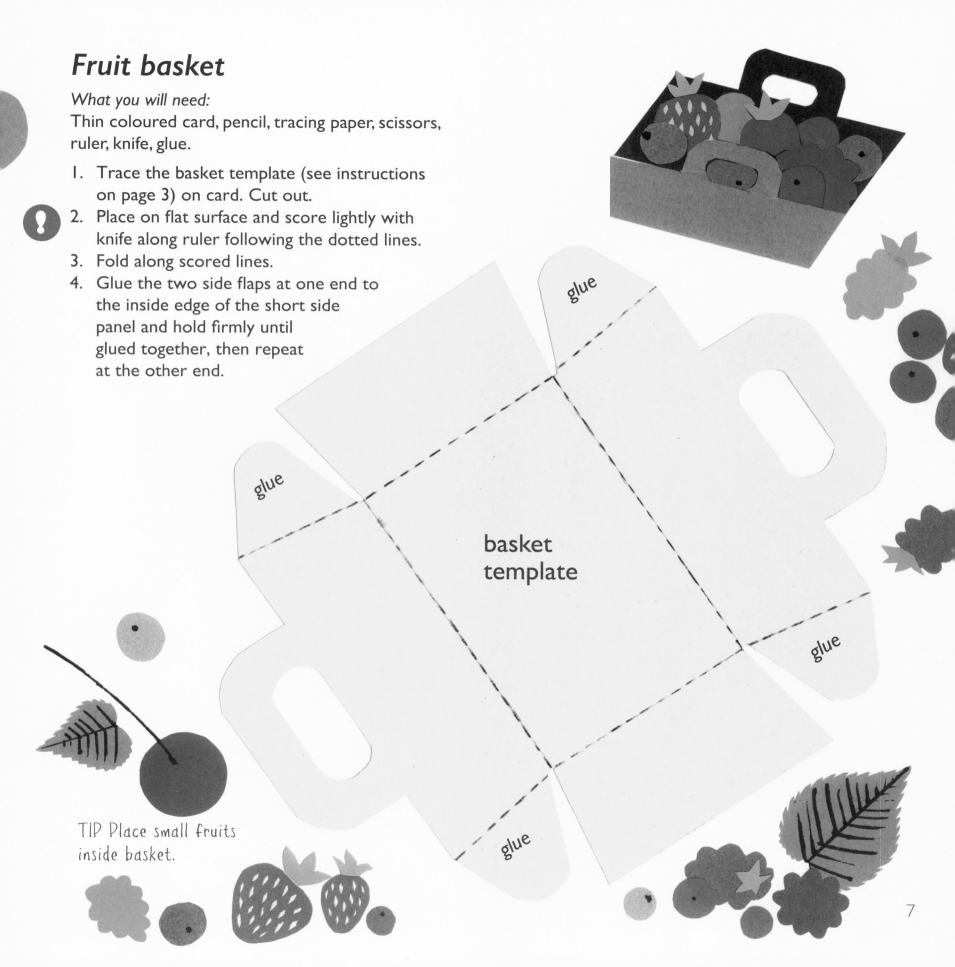

glue

glue

basket
template

glue

glue

TIP Place small fruits inside basket.

7

Proud Cats

baobab tree

termite mounds

pride of lions

agama lizard

Lions are large cats, nearly all of which live on the African grasslands with a small population surviving in India. The males have dark, long hair around their heads covering their neck, chest and shoulders, called a mane. They are a symbol for power, strength and ferocity and their roar can be heard from 5 miles (8 kilometres) away. Sadly lions are disappearing as their habitat decreases.

Lions are carnivores and they live in family groups called a pride. The females, just as ferocious as the males, hunt together catching zebra, gazelles and buffalos.

Lion's mane headdress

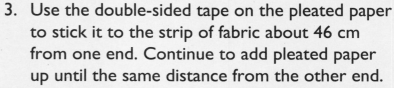

What you will need:
Brown and black paper, double-sided tape, strip of fabric approximately 3.5 cm wide and 132 cm long, pencil, tracing paper, scissors, glue.

1. Cut a strip of brown paper 16 cm wide and about 148 cm long. This is best in several lengths which can be roughly taped together once attached to the fabric strip.
2. Roughly pleat along edge of one piece of paper. Secure the pleating with double-sided tape.

3. Use the double-sided tape on the pleated paper to stick it to the strip of fabric about 46 cm from one end. Continue to add pleated paper up until the same distance from the other end.
4. Make ears by tracing (see instructions on page 3) the large outer part of the template four times on brown paper. Cut out and glue together to make two ears.
5. Trace the smaller inner part of the template twice on black paper and cut out. Glue on to ears.
6. Attach the ears to the fabric strip with tape 11 cm apart in the centre at the top.

pleating

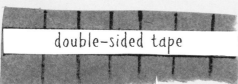

double-sided tape

Tear edge of paper into jagged points if you like

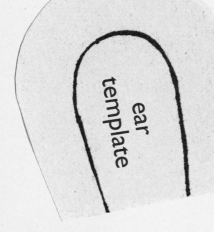

ear template

TIP Add some face paint and ROAR!

Arctic Hunters

iceberg

sea ice

seal

breathing hole

still hunting

Polar bears live in the Arctic Circle. Well adapted for life on the sea ice, their fur has two layers to keep them warm and they have bumps on the underneath of their paws to stop them from slipping. They are in danger of extinction due to global warming.

Excellent hunters, polar bears mostly eat seals, which they can smell from one mile (one and a half kilometres) away. They crouch for hours by breathing holes in the ice, waiting to pull the seal out when it comes up for air. They can swim for days to find food.

polar bear

snow cave

bear cubs

Frozen treats

None of these recipes uses an ice-cream maker.
They are very quick and easy to make.

Vanilla ice-cream

What you will need:
½ tin (387 g) sweetened condensed milk
300 ml double cream
1 tsp vanilla extract or essence

1. Put everything in a large bowl.
2. Beat until thick and quite stiff.
3. Place in an airtight container and freeze.
4. Remove about ten minutes before serving.

Strawberry lollies

What you will need:
250 g hulled strawberries
100 ml natural yoghurt
1 tsp honey
1 tsp vanilla extract or essence

1. Place everything in a blender and whizz until smooth.
2. Pour into four lolly moulds.
3. Freeze.

Frozen bananas

What you will need:
Bananas, sticks, hundreds and thousands, chopped nuts, chocolate.

1. Cut one end off banana or cut in half. Push in sticks.
2. Place on tray in freezer.
3. Melt chocolate in pan.
4. Dip bananas in chocolate and toppings. Freeze.

**WARNING –
NUT
ALLERGIES**

Do the same with pineapple rings!
Or simply freeze peeled bananas, remove
from freezer, whizz up in blender. Eat!

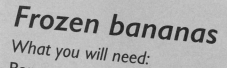
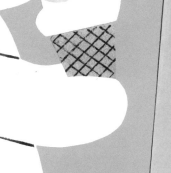

11

Endangered Bears

mountains

conifer tree

The giant panda is one of the most loved and protected endangered animals in the world. This large black and white bear is the symbol for the WWF (World Wildlife Fund).

Pandas have a very low birth rate and baby panda cubs are tiny, pink and blind when born. Adult pandas live alone in bamboo forests high in the mountains of south-western China where they are reliant on humans to protect their habitat. Despite being heavy, they are good climbers and eat as much as 13 kilograms (30 pounds) of bamboo each day.

panda

bamboo

Black and white patterns

The giant panda has a unique black and white patterned fur coat. Make your own patterns with these black and white squares cut into four.

What you will need:
Thin white card, black paper, glue, pair of compasses or small plate to draw around, ruler, pencil, scissors.

Here are some arrangements. Think of some more.

Make four squares with the same pattern and arrange into more patterns.

TIP: Do some reversing of the black and white.

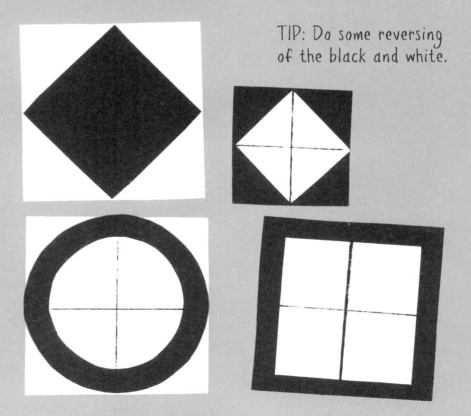

Creature Camouflage

tiger

grass

antelopes

acacia robusta tree

leopard

Some creatures use pattern and colour to make themselves hard to see. This is called camouflage. Humans hunt these creatures illegally for their patterned fur and skins.

Tigers, leopards and zebra rely on their distinctive, patterned coats, which help them to hide in their own habitat. The big cats use their camouflage to creep up unseen on their prey, while the zebra use their stripes to hide in the long grass from their predators. A group of zebra standing or moving together causes 'motion dazzle', their flickering stripes making it hard for predators to pick out one animal to kill.

Camouflaged animals

You can have fun placing the animals on patterned backgrounds. See how they disappear on some patterns and then stand out on others.

What you will need:
Several sheets of coloured and white paper, felt-tip pens OR paints and paintbrush, pencil, tracing paper, scissors.

1. Draw or paint three different patterns on sheets of paper. Yellow with black spots, orange with black stripes and white with black stripes.
2. Trace the animals (see instructions on page 3) and cut out of the appropriate pattern. Keep to edge of the paper so you have lots left.

3. Place animals on backgrounds. Does their camouflage work?

zebra template

leopard template

tiger template

15

Ancient Reptiles

zebras

impala

Crocodiles are semi-aquatic reptiles found in fresh and salt water in Africa, Asia, the Americas and Australia. They have thick, ridged scales on top, are smooth underneath and can swim fast. Their sharp teeth can be replaced up to fifty times in a lifetime. Crocodiles lay eggs in nests from which the babies emerge, in the same way as birds.

Submerged in the water, they wait to catch animals such as birds, mammals and other reptiles as they come to drink. Their excellent night vision gives them an advantage in the dark. They are very dangerous and even kill humans.

grasses

crocodiles

Egyptian plovers

Snapping crocodile

What you will need:
Stiff white paper, pencil, tracing paper, green paint, paintbrush, black felt-tip pen, scissors, one paper fastener.

1. Trace the two half crocodile templates (see instructions on page 3) on paper and cut out.
2. Place on a flat surface facing left and paint green leaving teeth and eye white.
3. When dry, add details in black felt-tip pen.

crocodile template

slit

slit

4. Place the top half on top of the bottom half matching the marks where the fastener goes. Push end of closed scissors through marks to make a small slit. Push fastener through then fold ends flat at the back.

SNAP SNAP!

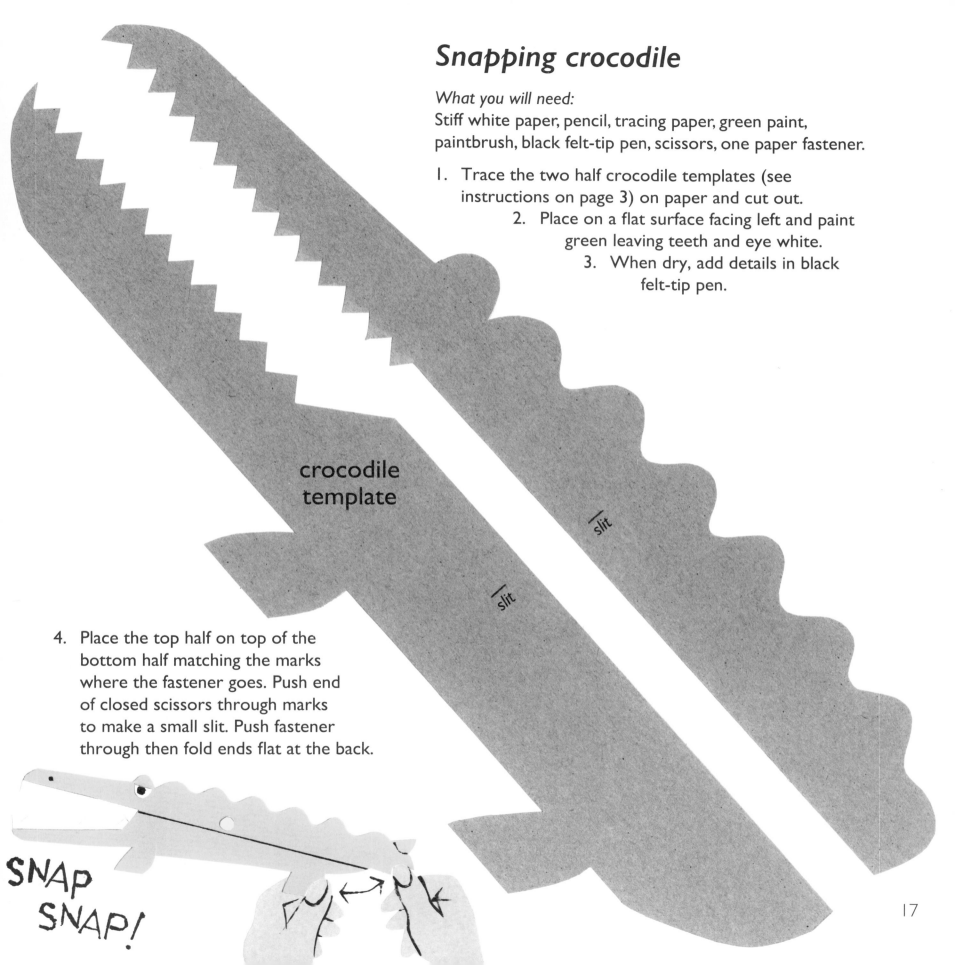

17

Jumping Joeys

kookaburra

Uluru

Kangaroos are native to Australia. They are marsupials, which means the female kangaroo has a pouch for her baby. This baby, called a joey, is born the size of a bean and crawls up into the pouch to feed and grow. After several months, they are ready to hop out and explore!

Kangaroos have powerful hind legs and large feet, which they use for hopping long distances and even swimming. Their strong tails help them balance. They are herbivores, feeding on grasses, flowers and leaves.

spinifex grass

kangaroos boxing

joey

pouch

Kangaroo hops

The perfect way to boost motor and coordination skills, build muscle strength and have fun at the same time!

Stair hop

Keeping your feet close together, hop up a small flight of stairs one at a time. Hop down again. This is quite a challenge so be careful.

Long jump

Mark on the ground with chalk if outside or with tape if inside. One line for the start then more lines about 13 cm apart. See how far you can jump.

Hopscotch

Chalk this number grid on a pavement or playground. Hop on one leg from 1 to 9 then turn around and hop back. You can put both feet down on the squares that are side by side, if you like.

Hoppety hop

Hold a soft foam ball between knees whilst standing. Hop along keeping ball in place.

One-foot hops

Lift one knee, jump standing on other leg. Repeat on other leg.

Sack race

Use a sack, old pillowcase or bin liner and have a race jumping along.

Frog hops

Cut out paper lily pads. Place on ground and jump from one to another.

TIP: Don't forget skipping!

Spiky Rodents

North American porcupine

Porcupines are slow-moving rodents covered in thirty thousand long, sharp spines called quills. They rattle their quills when agitated or to frighten off predators as well as clattering their teeth. If they lose any quills, they grow back. Babies are born with soft quills which soon harden. A mother and baby together are known as a prickle!

In the continents of Africa and Asia, the porcupines are large and nocturnal. In the Americas, they are smaller, not strictly nocturnal and climb trees. They are herbivores, eating bark, leaves, grass and berries.

African feather grass

African crested porcupine

Malaysian porcupine

Potato porcupines

What you will need:
Large potato, knife, black paint, paintbrush, wooden toothpicks, two cloves.

1. Cut slice off potato so it does not move about.

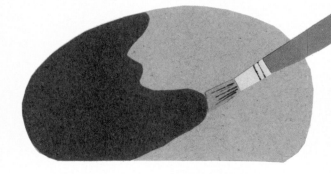

2. Paint potato in thick black paint. Leave to dry.
3. Paint stripes on the toothpicks. Leave to dry.

4. Push the toothpicks into the potato facing away from the head end.
5. Push cloves into face for eyes.

TIP: Place porcupine in shallow saucer of cold water to make it last longer. It will shrivel eventually.

Make a 'prickle' by adding a baby porcupine. Use a small potato and break the toothpicks in half.

21

Big-beaked Birds

choco toucan

toco toucan

The toco toucan lives in South America and is the largest and best known of the toucan family. They live in holes in trees, where they lay their eggs once a year. They have a noisy, harsh call and can live for up to twenty years.

They have huge, colourful beaks, which look very heavy but are actually made of a light material with a honeycomb structure. Their beaks have a serrated edge, perfect for reaching for fruit, insects, frogs and small birds.

channel-billed toucan

rainbow toucan

Toucan tree house

What you will need:
Card tube (like one from kitchen towel), scissors, stiff white paper, pencil, tracing paper, paints, paintbrush, tissue paper, glue.

1. Cut hole in the tube about a third of the way from top.
2. Trace the toucan template (see instructions on page 3) and cut two from the white paper including the slit.
3. Paint both sides of the toucans leaving one side to dry before painting the other side.
4. Tear pieces of tissue paper and glue to tree trunk.
5. Finally perch the toucans, one on top and one in the hole.

toucan
template

slit

Super Snakes

blue viper

rattlesnake

Snakes are long, legless reptiles that lay eggs. The longest are pythons, measuring up to 9 metres (28 feet) in length. The shortest are thread snakes, measuring around 10 centimetres (4 inches). There are about three thousand different types living all over the world apart from some islands like Antarctica, Ireland, Greenland and New Zealand where there are none.

Their flexible jaws allow them to swallow creatures much larger than themselves. Some snakes are venomous and can kill their prey in one bite! Snakes smell through their forked tongues.

snakes hatching from eggs

milk snake

cobra

Spiralling snakes

Make lots of these in different sizes, colours and patterns.
If you hang them by an open window, they will sway about.

What you will need:
Coloured paper, paints, paintbrush, pencil, scissors,
needle, thread, sticky tape.

1. Paint patterns on the paper and leave to dry.
2. Turn over and draw a curled up snake in pencil
   on the back.

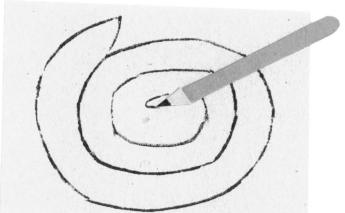

3. Cut out along line.
4. Turn over and draw eyes on head.
5. Thread needle, knot end and push
   through head, secure knot with sticky
   tape underneath. Hang up.

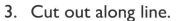

Decorate coloured
snake with pens

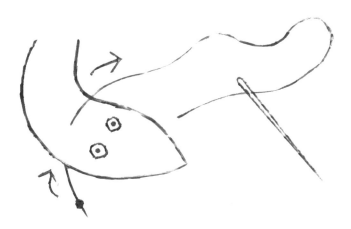

25

The Tallest Animal

acacia trees

giraffes

acacia leaf

acacia flowers

Giraffes have very long legs and necks and a unique coat pattern. They live across the continent of Africa and are the tallest animal on Earth. As herbivores, they use their height and long tongues to pull off leaves, fruit and flowers from trees. A group of giraffes is called a tower.

The male bulls fight to prove who is strongest by hitting each other with their necks until one gives up and walks away. Lions, hyenas and other large predators hunt and eat them. Giraffes spend most of their life standing including giving birth so the baby has a long way to fall to the ground!

Patchwork giraffe

What you will need:

Thin coloured card, pencil, tracing paper, patterned papers, glue, scissors, black felt-tip pen.

1. Trace giraffe template (see instructions on page 3) on card.
2. Trace small pentagon following same instructions as above on card and cut out.
3. Place pentagon on patterned papers. Draw around it and cut out.
4. Glue pentagon shapes on giraffe leaving gap between each overlapping outline. Leave head, tail and legs clear.
5. Cut out giraffe.

pentagon templates

6. Draw details on giraffe in black felt-tip pen.

TIP: Draw your own larger giraffe and use larger pentagon shapes.

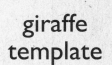

giraffe template

The River Horse

grey
heron

The common hippopotamus, or hippo, lives in eastern Africa and its much smaller cousin, the pygmy hippo, lives in forests in western Africa. The name comes from the ancient Greek meaning 'river horse'.

Making their home in slow-moving rivers, lakes and swamps, hippos mate, give birth, sleep and fight in the water but they cannot actually swim. Instead they hold their breath and walk along the bottom. They stay submerged up to their ears, eyes and nostrils for much of the day, coming out at night to graze on grass. Hippos are very aggressive and unpredictable making them incredibly dangerous.

oxpeckers

hippos

mud

water
hyacinth

Hidden hippo

Here are some ideas for creating pictures of a hippo in water with just the top of their head showing.

What you will need:
Coloured paper including some grey paper, scissors, pencil, tracing paper, glitter, coloured pencils OR paints and paintbrush, glue.

1. Trace the hippo template (see instructions on page 3) on grey paper and cut out.
2. Glue on coloured paper.

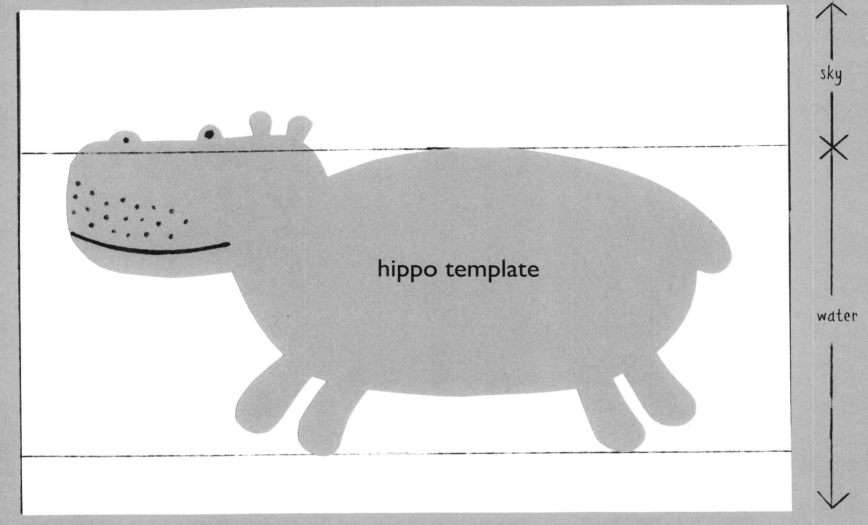

hippo template

sky

water

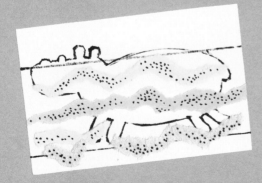

Draw waves in glue over hippo and sprinkle with glitter.

Glue tracing paper over hippo and colour with watery patterns.

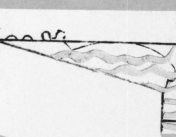

Make a card with the top part cut off at the water level. Open to see the whole hippo. Decorate the front.

29

Eagle

harpy eagle

African fish eagle

Eagles are large, powerful birds of prey. They have huge wingspans, large hooked beaks, strong legs and talons. There are over sixty different species.

Their excellent eyesight helps them to spot their prey from long distances. As they soar and glide through the skies, they hunt fish, snakes and small mammals. An eagle's nest is called an eyrie and eagles build them at the top of tall trees or high cliffs returning each year to lay their eggs and rear their young.

golden eagle

bald eagle

chicks

Eagle eye 'I spy'

Make a chart, or ask someone to make one for you, with a list of things to spot when you go out. It can be a list of natural things or of man-made things. Tick off when you spot them. Were there other things you did not expect to see?

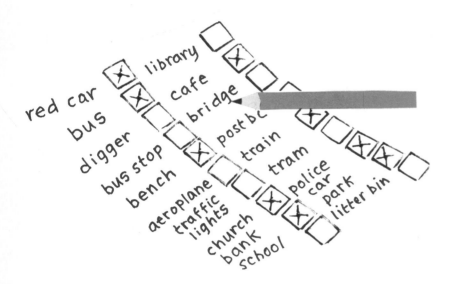

One tree

Take a long, careful look at just one thing, such as a tree. With a sheet of paper, crayons and pens, record what you see. What is it? How big is it? Can you touch the top or reach all around it? Does it have any leaves, flowers, twigs or fruit on it? Can you spot any insects on it? Make a bark rubbing.

Eagle eye

This is a great outdoor game for a few children, best played in an area with trees, bushes and undergrowth. First, create a 'nest' about three and a half metres across with an edge made of sticks, pinecones or clothes. The 'eagle' (an adult or older child) stands in the nest, closes their eyes and slowly counts to ten whilst the children hide. The 'eagle' calls 'the eagle is awake!' and without moving tries to spot the hiding children, who must be looking at the 'eagle'. When spotted, the child comes into the nest and can pretend to be prey, birds, rabbits or fish. Afterwards, the eagle counts to ten and this time the children can move towards the nest just three paces each time. Continue until everyone has been spotted or reached the nest unseen. The last one wins!

31

brown rat

arrow-poison frog

Glossary

These difficult words appear in the book.
Here is what they mean.

breeding – producing baby animals

carnivore – eats mostly or only meat

extinction – disappearing completely
from earth

flexible – able to stretch far without breaking

habitat – natural home

herbivore – eats only plants

nocturnal – active at night-time

poaching – taking illegally, often killing
animals

pollution – to spoil with dangerous substances

pouch – a cosy pocket at the front of the
animal which contains nipples from which
the baby can feed on milk

predator – carnivorous hunters

prey – a creature hunted by predators

reptile – cold-blooded vertebrate (having a
bony skeleton and a well developed brain)
covered in scales or plates and laying eggs
with their young inside

serrated – saw-like edge

unique – unlike anything else

venomous – able to inject venom, which causes
harm and maybe even death

orchid

Published by b small publishing ltd.

First published in 2021 by b small publishing ltd.

Wild Book   ISBN 978-1-912909-30-8   www.bsmall.co.uk

text and illustrations © b small publishing 2021

Editorial: Sam Hutchinson   Design: Louise Millar   Printed in China by WKT Co. Ltd.

1 2 3 4 5 6 7 8 9

British Library Cataloguing-in-Publication Data:
A catalogue record for this book is available from the British Library.

armadillo